Making the Most of Your Time

Bishop Timothy J. Clarke

Making the Most of Your Time!

ISBN 978-0-9764022-4-4

Powerful Purpose Publishing
P O Box 32132
Columbus, OH 43232

Publishing Consultant: Obieray Rogers (www.rubiopublishing.com)

Printed in the United States of America.

Table of Contents

This book is dedicated to the men in my life who are my brothers and my friends. You know who you are and I pray that you know what you mean to me. You have helped me to make my time count.

This book is also dedicated to the people of God at First Church of God in Far Rockaway, New York, both here and in heaven. My time started with you. I am what I am because God placed me among you.

Introduction

YOUR LIFE IS COMPRISED of seasons; once you understand that, you are on your way to becoming everything that God wants you to be. However, in order to embrace this concept you must first believe there is a purpose for your life.

You have a God who directs your life and orders your steps and even when bad things happen, He is able to make it work together for your good. Nothing that happens, whether good or bad, comes in your life without the inspection and approval of Almighty God who loves you, knows you, and has plans for you.

If you can't believe that, then this book won't make any sense to you. You have to believe there is a purpose for your life, there is a reason for your existence, and that God is not randomly letting things happen to you. A mature Christian doesn't only thank God for those places of ease and comfort, but also for the problems and challenges. A mature Christian knows that challenges are a blessing from God, because God has a purpose for your life and nothing just happens.

You will only make the most of your time when you understand the seasons of silence and suffering that God allows. Both seasons are vital and necessary to your Christian growth and will help you in *Making the Most of Your Time!*

PART ONE

THE SILENT YEARS

Chapter One
The Season of Silence

GOD HAS DESIGNED YOUR life to have purpose and rhythm, and each phase of your life is building on something and leading somewhere. You need to remember this truth: God is in no rush to make you. He will do whatever He has to, and take whatever time is necessary, to make you what He wants you to be. God is in no hurry and takes you through a season of time I call the silent years.

The silent years are those years when no one knows you, no one calls you, and no one uses you. You are doing nothing great for God because you are in a holding pattern. It is in those years that God is making, shaping, and molding you for His glory and ultimate use. These are not wasted years.

The silent years are used for training and preparation. God uses these years to get you ready for what He wants you to do. A study of the Bible reveals that every person God used had a period of silence: Moses—great lawgiver and emancipator—spent forty years in the desert. David—anointed king—went back to tending sheep. Joseph had dreams, was thrown in a well and prison, and it would take seventeen years for the dreams to come true. Before God uses you greatly He will put you in a place of solitude and silence. It is during this time that God will do His greatest internal work and prepare you for what He is going to do later.

As I reflected on what the Holy Spirit has said about the silent years, I realized that God is not mad at or angry with us. However, during this period of inactivity we sometimes begin to wonder, "What's wrong with me?" The silent years are not an indicator of God's anger, but rather an indicator of the plan, purpose, and will of God. God never takes us higher without taking us deeper. The job of excavating and moving stuff out of our lives is sometimes a laborious and extended process. The bigger we are, the longer it takes to get rid of the clutter and junk. God has not forgotten or abandoned us. It is during this period that God is doing the most effective and productive work He will ever do. If we don't learn how to accept this period, phase, and place of God, we will never be what God wants us to be.

ANOINTING AND PREPARATION

God can and will anoint only what you give Him. So many people have made shipwrecks of their ministry or calling and have fallen short of their potential, because the anointing is no substitute for preparation.

I don't want to be in church with a choir, preachers, or saints that are not anointed. When my back's against the wall and I am between the devil and the deep blue sea, I don't need somebody talking loud and saying nothing when my soul is in trouble and my life is a mess. I need somebody with some anointing who can bring about a change in my life. I believe in the anointing, but the anointing is no substitute for preparation. The anointing is not flashy, showy, or pretentious. The anointing is calm, yet powerful, and it never brings glory to a person; it always brings glory to God.

I want people anointed, but the anointing will only be effective to our degree of preparation. I spend hours on my knees studying, researching, and seeking to understand what a passage of Scripture means because I want to be prepared when I stand to preach. Once I know I have done my best and prepared, then I have the right to say that God anoints me. It is amazing what happens when preparation meets opportunity.

YOUR IMPACT WILL BE DETERMINED
BY HOW YOU HANDLE THE SILENT YEARS

How you handle the silent years determines if and when you go to the next level. If you push yourself to the next level, you will never succeed or have staying power because the pressure will be more than you can handle. Don't be a shooting star that blazes for a minute and is then gone.

I have been the Senior Pastor of First Church of God for over thirty years. When I arrived in Columbus, Ohio we had just a few members and I remember watching other churches grow and wondered why we didn't. God showed me that I wouldn't have been able to handle the growth then that we have now. I would have been intimidated and would have relied on people instead of God. God let me go through the silent years so that when the growth occurred I wouldn't be impressed. I know who brought, kept, anointed, and blessed me, and that is God. I can and must depend on Him to make it.

God took every person He used through a season of silence. He took them to a place where He covered them and hid them away. He took them through the silent years.

Chapter Two
First Things First

TRYING TO ESCAPE THE silent years will mean that your life will never be as effective or enduring as God planned. A life that is going to have impact and make an impression must have a solid and deep foundation. We don't like the silent years because we are not allowed to do much; it is a period of God-ordained inactivity. As a matter of fact, in the silent years it is not about what we are doing, but about what God is doing in us. One of the great tragedies of life is that so many people miss this phase. They avoid it, run past it, or try to ignore it. Their lives soon show the effects of not going through the silent years, because they run into something they can't handle and crash and burn. Jesus Christ shows us how to handle the silent years:

> *Every year His parents went to Jerusalem for the Feast of the Passover. When He was twelve years old, they went up to the Feast, according to the custom. After the Feast was over, while His parents were returning home,*

the boy Jesus stayed behind in Jerusalem, but they were unaware of it. Thinking He was in their company, they traveled on for a day. Then they began looking for Him among their relatives and friends. When they did not find Him, they went back to Jerusalem to look for Him. After three days they found Him in the temple courts, sitting among the teachers, listening to them and asking them questions. Everyone who heard Him was amazed at His understanding and His answers. When His parents saw Him, they were astonished. His mother said to Him, "Son, why have you treated us like this? Your father and I have been anxiously searching for you." "Why were you searching for me?" He asked. "Didn't you know I had to be in my father's house?" but they did not understand what He was saying to them. Then He went down to Nazareth with them and was obedient to them. But His mother treasured all these things in her heart. And Jesus grew in wisdom and stature, and in favor with God and men. (Luke 2:41-52)

Some people read the Bible chronologically and think that since Jesus was twelve in chapter two then chapter three must take place the next day, week, month, or year. We need to understand that between chapters two and three are eighteen years of silence! Jesus didn't heal one sick person; He didn't preach one sermon, and He didn't do one miracle. He experienced eighteen years of inactivity and of being behind the scenes.

Do you know what I find so incredible about this? Jesus was as much the Son of God at twelve as He was at thirty. The same power that He used to open blinded eyes at thirty, He had at twelve. The same anointing to raise the dead that He had at thirty, He had at twelve. The same power to feed multitudes that He had at thirty, He had at twelve. However, at twelve He learned how to harness His power; to be disciplined, submitted, and wait His turn. When I realized that Jesus had the same power and anointing at twelve that He had at thirty, I was blown away.

You may be familiar with the books of the Apocrypha. Someone asked me why I don't preach from those books and I told them some of those books have Jesus playing with a clay bird and turning it into a real bird; Jesus raising one of His playmates who died back to life or Jesus striking playmates with lightning when He didn't get His way. These extra biblical books add things that the canon of Scripture doesn't record. The reason I reject them is because they deny a basic premise: At age twelve Jesus would have the same power He would have at thirty, however, He also had the ability to harness it and to discipline Himself so He never used it.

We don't hear from Jesus for eighteen years. He is sweeping the floor in Joseph's carpentry shop, raking leaves, and drawing water from the well. What amazes me is that the Man who made the water is now drawing water and the Man who made the leaves is raking leaves. Jesus understood the significance of His silent season. I wish I could get you to understand that where you are right now may not be your season to shine; it may be your season to be silent. If Jesus had to experience this season, surely you have to experience it, too. You need to allow God to shape, make, and prepare you for whatever He has for you, and that preparation is done in the silent years.

"After three days they found him in the temple courts, sitting among the teachers, listening to them and asking them questions" (Luke 2:46). We get caught up in the fact that Jesus was sitting with the elders conversing, but I get excited about Luke 2:51. I believe in between the lines, *"Why were you searching for me?" He asked. "Didn't you know I had to be in my Father's house?"* (Luke 2:49) and *"Then He went down to Nazareth with*

them and was obedient to them" (Luke 2:51) some dialogue was left out. Keep in mind it took three days for Mary and Joseph to find Him so you know they weren't happy about it. There was probably more dialogue then what is quoted, but the Holy Ghost wouldn't let it be recorded. Regardless of whatever else was said, Jesus went home to Nazareth and was subject to His parents. Loosely translated He went home and acted like He had some sense and never pulled that stunt again.

I am not diminishing what He did in the temple; I am trying to show you that even though He is the Son of God, He had to live His life based on the seasons and phases of time that all of us have. In spite of being older than His mother and father (since He existed before them), in this phase of His life He had to act like a child and go through what every other child goes through.

During His silent years Jesus teaches us some powerful lessons. I know you're on fire and want to turn the world upside down, but you're never going to be your best, realize your fullest potential, or accomplish all that God wants until you learn how to function in this phase of your life.

OBEDIENCE

Jesus didn't argue with His parents when they went back to get Him. He didn't point out that He was the Son of God and could stay in the temple. Joseph said it was time to go and Jesus obeyed.

You need to understand that what messed us up in the first place was disobedience. That is what Adam and Eve did in the Garden—they disobeyed God. Each of us has an innate proclivity that bends toward disobedience. Our parents told us not to do something and the very thing they told us not to do is exactly what we did. As adults we haven't gotten better and I can prove it. We know that the speed limit is fifty-five or sixty-five, so why do we drive seventy-five or eighty? Because there is something in us that refuses to obey. We don't care what God or the police say; there is something in our nature that bends toward disobedience.

God knows you will never be all He wants until you learn to obey. He allows the silent years to teach you obedience. God will make you take the class over and over until you learn this lesson. If this were school, you would still be in the third grade at sixty years old! Here is how you know you are ready to graduate:

- You obey willingly and no one has to force you.

- You obey fully and don't just do enough to get by.

- You obey joyfully without grumbling and com- plaining.

SUBMISSION

In the silent years God will teach you how to submit. Obedience is different from submission. Obedience is something that you can be made to do, but no one can make you submit.

Nazi concentration camp survivor Victor Frankel wrote about his decision to never submit to his captors although he would obey them, in spite of all the horrendous hatred in the camp.

Many of my forbearers had to obey under the lash and whip of slavery, but they never submitted. Slaves understood that people can make you obey, but no one can make you submit, because submission is an attitude.

God will not make you submit to Him. Submission is an act of your will and an attitude of worship.

- You must submit to the wisdom of God because He knows more than you do.

- You must submit to the way of God which is how He is working in your life.

- You must submit to the will of God being done in your life.

When you understand the wisdom, way, and will of God, and know all of that is working together for your good, you have no trouble submitting to Him. You know He knows best, He has a plan for your life, and He knows the way He is leading you.

GROWTH

"And Jesus grew in wisdom and stature, and in favor with God and men" (Luke 2:52). This is the balanced life God wants you to have. Jesus increased in wisdom (mentally), stature (physically), favor with God (spiritually), and favor with men (socially). Every area of His life was well-balanced because God does not want you coming out of the silent years warped, twisted, or perverted.

God will be looking for balance when He gets ready to use you. Do you wonder why God isn't using you right now? Perhaps it's because He knows you aren't ready. God has a plan for your life and He is in no hurry to get it done. He is not in a race against time. He knows His will for you.

God is not going to send you out unprepared once opportunity comes your way. You have issues and rough edges that God is trying to smooth off and correct. If He sends you out too early, you will do more harm than good. God knows some of you still hurt from a divorce so you don't need to counsel anyone yet. If you start counseling now, all of the hatred and bitterness from the divorce will spill out in the session. God has called some of you to preach, just not right now. You are still dealing with all of the baggage from your past. If you preach now, you will spew venom throughout the congregation.

God gives you the silent years to be with Him so He can work on you before He sends you out. He wants you to look at the messy stuff of your life and deal with it positively. Then you can testify, "It was ugly and painful, but God healed me, and if He healed me, He can heal you." "Yes I've failed, but God picked me up and gave me another chance. If He did it for me, He can do it for you." You don't learn that until you get by yourself with God. You thought you had something to say and a job to do, but He has put you on hold until He can get you ready.

17

God knows where He is taking you and what He is doing in your life. If you trust Him, He will bring you to where He wants you to be.

CLEARED FOR TAKE OFF

Several months ago I was in Chicago trying to get back to my church for a meeting. The plane was boarded and sitting on the runway, however, we couldn't leave right away because there were other planes ahead of us. We sat and sat and sat. I was beginning to get upset until the Lord told me to be still and learn something from this incident. God began to show me a theological truth sitting on the runway. We were on a real airplane with a real pilot who was qualified to get us in the air, but it wasn't our turn to take off.

During the silent years you may feel like you're on an airplane sitting on the runway; you're poised and ready to go, the crew and passengers are on board, but you can't go until the other planes take off. Everybody else seems to be taking off before you. But guess what? God is in the control tower, and if you will learn to wait, then you won't jump out of line and mess up the order and plan of God.

You need the silent years for preparation. I understand the value of the silent years. I remember the day God called me to preach. I was a teenager and it was dinnertime at my spiritual father's house, the late Dr. James E. Cray. I eagerly told him I believed the Lord had called me to preach. He said, "All right" and kept right on eating. I said, "Did you hear me?" and he said, "Yes. I'll keep it in mind," and kept right on eating. A few months later he wanted me to read the Scripture at Wednesday night service and said, "Stand by the communion table and don't say anything about the Scripture. Just read it and sit down," and that is what I did.

Dad Cray didn't allow me to do anything else for several months. One day he told me I was to give a trial sermon and said, "Don't preach too long or try and talk beyond your experience. Just say a little word and sit down." I gave the sermon, the saints shouted, and I thought I was a preacher. He then said, "This first year you don't go anywhere to preach. Don't accept any invitations. You'll preach at home and that way if you mess up, it's here at home." I submitted to him for that year.

The following year he told me he was going to let me go away to preach, but I wasn't to take an offering anywhere I went. If they gave me an offering, I was to bring it to him because he didn't want me to start out preaching for money. I thought he had two horns and a tail by this time and kept thinking, "Doesn't he know I'm anointed?"

My church was having an annual choir day and they wanted me to be the master of ceremonies and Dad Cray said no. They told me what he said and I asked him why he wouldn't let me do the assignment. He said, "Because these people act like you're the only one around that can do anything. People will build you up and swell your head and the moment you mess up they'll walk away from you. You're a good preacher, and one day you'll be a great preacher because the hand of God is on you, but I have to make sure you understand what ministry is all about." I thought he was so mean and was trying to hold me back. Instead Dad Cray was making me go through my silent years of inactivity and being unknown so that when God loosed me I could handle it. I now look back on that experience with a very grateful heart.

I know you're full of energy and the anointing of God is on you, but right now it's not about the anointing, it's about your attitude. God will never use you if you don't learn how to obey, submit, and grow. Jesus grew in wisdom, stature, and favor from God and men. He was balanced.

It is during the silent years that God does His greatest work. There are things that God will only do in this season. You can't avoid the silent years or run from them, so calm down and let God work. Sooner than you think you will hear Him say, "You are now cleared for takeoff."

Chapter Three
Sand in the Hourglass

ONLY GOD KNEW ALL THAT would happen on September 11, 2001. Having now lived through the horror of that day I believe all of us have a new appreciation and understanding for the words of Moses in Psalm 90:12, *"Teach us to number our days aright, that we may gain a heart of wisdom."* There is no doubt that since September 11, 2001 the prayer of Moses has now become the prayer of most saints. It is almost as if all of us have a new sense of urgency and we are praying, "God help me make the most of my time." September 11, 2001 reminds us that we can take nothing for granted. Life is precious and a gift from God and only God can show us how to use our time wisely.

When I was a little boy, my grandmother took in laundry as a way to earn money and keep an eye on all of her grandchildren. One of her favorite pastimes was watching soap operas, especially *Days of Our Lives*. Each episode opened with a large hourglass appearing on the screen and then the voice-over, "Like sand in the hourglass, so are the days of our lives."

September 11, 2001 and current events remind us that indeed our lives are like sand in an hourglass.

YOUR LIFE IS FRAGILE

Your life and times are fragile. You must handle life with care and prayer. If you try to do things on your own, you will soon discover you are not wise enough or strong enough to handle what life will bring your way. That is why David said, *"As surely as the Lord lives and as you live, there is only a step between me and death"* (1 Samuel 20:3). In other words, you can be here today and gone today. There is a fragile nature to life and the only way you can handle it is to turn your life over to God.

YOUR DAYS ARE FEW

The days of your life are few. I know some of you feel you're going to live forever and that time is on your side. This is particularly true of those who are young; they tend to feel they are invincible and that nothing can stop, hurt, or slow them down. Take it from someone who has been around the block a few times, even if you live to be a hundred, your days are few when compared to eternity: *"Man born of woman is of a few days and full of trouble"* (Job 14:1). It seems that no sooner does one problem end before another one crops up. It seems that no sooner do you handle one crisis then life brings something else unexpected.

If you put your life in the hands of God, it doesn't matter what life brings your way. There is a God who sits on the throne and all power is in His hands.

YOUR DAYS ARE FLEETING

Time is moving quickly. Remember when you were a child and it seemed as if Christmas would never come? Remember right around the end of September, first of October, you would start counting down the days until Christmas? Every day seemed like a year, but not anymore.

Birthdays were the same way. On the eve of turning thirteen I stayed up until midnight so that I could watch myself turn thirteen. I stood at the mirror to see if I would grow a mustache, develop instant muscles, and have automatic sex appeal. Two minutes after midnight I still didn't have a mustache or muscles, I was still a geek, and the girls weren't thinking about me! I couldn't wait until I was thirteen and then sixteen and then eighteen and then twenty-one. I want to testify today that if I could find a way to slow down and bottle up time I would.

Time is fleeting and it doesn't wait on anyone. You don't have time to waste or play, so you need to make up your mind to serve God and give Him the best years of your life.

The days of your life are fragile, few, and fleeting. You need wisdom that only comes from God to make the most of the time you have.

Chapter Four
Spread, Shape, and Mold

CEMENT IS FLUID WHEN poured and a contractor will tell you that as long as it is wet it can be spread, shaped, or molded. In the silent years, you are flexible, shapeable, fluid, and liquid so before you get set in your ways God can speak to you. There are three things God puts in you:

CHARACTER

Some of you are running after skill and God is looking for character. Before God will utilize your skill He is going to develop your character. He is going to shape you into a person of integrity who pays your bills on time, lives within your means, and keeps your zippers up and your skirts down. Character is what defines you. It is also what determines your boundaries, absolutes, and limits. Power and authority in a person without character is a dangerous thing.

SKILL

God is an intelligent God to be served with your mind, body, and spirit. You were born with at least one talent and at your second birth you were given at least one spiritual gift. It is your assignment to develop and nurture both your talents and gifts so that God gets optimum performance out of you. You must always strive to become better at what you do.

MATURITY

God matures you to handle what comes your way, both good and bad. God will bring you to a place where nothing impresses or crushes you. You are balanced. Maturity has nothing to do with age. It is not chronological, but experiential. Maturity has a settling quality in that you are neither impressed nor intimidated by what life brings your way. You face it knowing that God is in control. Another word for maturity is stability because it secures you so you're not easily moved.

ARE YOU BUILDING A SKYSCRAPER
OR A CHICKEN COUP?

The footer of a building determines the strength of the foundation, and the foundation determines the size of the building. A building can never be bigger than its foundation. You can't have a three-foot foundation, two inches deep and expect to build a skyscraper. You can build a chicken coop, but you won't build a skyscraper. Matter of fact, any builder will tell you the higher you plan to go up the deeper you have to go down. You cannot go higher than you have gone deeper. The silent years are your foundational years where God puts something in you. Can I tell you what God wants to put in you?

HUMILITY

The silent years teach you humility. When you come out of this season, you will not be stuck on yourself. You may go in like you have a stick stuck up your back, but you will come out changed.

TEACHABLENESS

In the silent years God will teach you things you will never learn at any other time. You are in school during the silent years. God starts writing on the blackboard of your life the lessons He wants you to use the rest of your days.

ACCOUNTABILITY

Everybody is accountable to somebody, even Jesus. That is proven in the verse: *"Then He went down to Nazareth with them and was obedient to them"* (Luke 2:51).

If humility, teachableness, and accountability are not in your life, God wants to use the silent years to pour them into you. He can never exalt or promote you until He has put these things inside you. As long as no one can tell you anything or you won't submit yourself to anyone, God will leave you on the shelf.

Chapter Five
Separated At Birth

I WANT TO EXAMINE the life of Paul to help us understand the silent season.

BIOLOGICAL SEPARATION

Paul said there are two distinct periods of separation. The first occurs at birth: *"But when God, who set me apart from birth and called me by His grace. . ."* (Galatians 1:15). The first real separation took place before you were born. God wrote your biography and literally separated you before birth for where He plans for you to go. You thought that your call to preach, sing, or serve was your first call. No! If the Bible is right (and it is), your first call came before you were born: *"Before I formed you in the womb I knew you, before you were born I set you apart"* (Jeremiah 1:5).

I read an interview with an author who made an interesting statement. The interviewer asked what was the hardest thing about writing a novel and the author replied keeping the characters in check. The author has to know where the characters are going because sometimes they develop a life of their own. No matter what plot changes occurs, the author is never under a burden because he knows where the characters are going. That sounds like God who is the Author of your life. Even though your plot changes and you don't know all that is going on, nothing catches God by surprise. God knew the direction your life would take before you were born. God doesn't get nervous when the plot changes. He just keeps directing you because He knows where He plans for you to go from the moment of your birth.

God has a plan for your life. Your life has a purpose that began in eternity. God didn't create you and on the day you were born wonder what He was going to do with you. That is what you do; you look at what has happened and wonder how you are going to handle it. That is not what God does. God had to create you to fulfill what was on His mind before you were born. Your purpose is not in response to your being here; your being here is in response to His plan and purpose. In other words, God does not operate from the present to the future; He operates from the future back to the present.

You were in the mind of God from the beginning of creation. Since God knows everything, He didn't learn anything today that He didn't already know in the beginning. That is why when you pray you aren't telling

God something He doesn't already know. Put your hand over your heart and repeat this affirmation: "I was on God's mind in the beginning. I am not an accident or a mistake." When God decided to populate the earth, you were one He decided to let live. Do you know how many babies have been stillborn or aborted? God planned you from the beginning. Paul said *"He separated me from my mother's womb,"* which means nothing that happens in your life is without purpose, even the bad things.

SPIRITUAL SEPARATION

The second period of separation occurs at the time of commissioning: *"But when God was pleased to reveal His Son in me so that I might preach Him among the Gentiles..."* (Galatians 1:16). God separates you for a work. He lays His hand on you for teaching, preaching, singing, witnessing, evangelizing, helps, administration, prophecy, or any number of gifts, offices, ministries, or functions. After God has prepared you, He then lays His hand on you and sets you apart for work. The time of separation is painful and difficult because it takes you out of your comfort zone.

You are separated from the life you had before Christ:

> *For you have heard of my previous way of life in Judaism, how intensely I persecuted the church of God and tried to destroy it.* (Galatians 1:13)

You are separated from your traditions, opinions, and teachings:

> *I was advancing in Judaism beyond many Jews my own age and was extremely zealous for the traditions of my fathers.* (Galatians 1:14)

You are separated from people:

> *But when God, who set me apart from birth and called me by His grace, was pleased to reveal His Son in me so that I might preach Him among the Gentiles, I did not consult any man, nor did I go up to Jerusalem to see those who were apostles before I was, but I went immediately into Arabia and later returned to Damascus.* (Galatians 1:15–17)

God separates you from your past, traditions, and people. If you are not willing to be separated, you are never going to do anything great for God. You will only achieve greatness to the degree you are willing to let go of something. Whatever you let go of, God will multiply more back into your life.

What are you holding onto? Is it job security? As long as you hold onto that job you're never going to start your own business. Yes, it is a paycheck, but what is a paycheck when your destiny waits for you? Yes, it is security, but what is security when the purpose of God is right beyond the door? What is job security, insurance, or a pension when God is calling you to do something that has never been done before? You will never achieve greatness and true satisfaction until you are willing to take a risk with God. You need to let go of what you already have to lay claim to what God has for you.

LESSONS FROM THE LIFE OF PAUL

In Galatians chapter one Paul allows you a glimpse into his life and reminds you of some basic truths:

Timothy J. Clarke

YOU HAD A LIFE BEFORE CHRIST

Paul helps you understand that you had a life before Jesus and that seldom, if ever, was that life very pretty. I know you're deep now and all the gifts reside in you, but you haven't been saved all of your life. You try to pretend like you have walked with Jesus all of your life but, *"All have sinned and fall short of the glory of God"* (Romans 3:23). You weren't born knowing Jesus Christ. You have a past and skeletons in the closet. You have things in your life that you are ashamed of, embarrassed by, and pray that no one else finds out about. Aren't you glad the blood of Jesus Christ covers you? You are clean because of the grace of God, the love of God, and the blood of Jesus.

YOU HAD STRUGGLES IN THE BEGINNING

Paul also helps you understand that you struggled in the early days of your Christian walk and you can't pretend that you didn't. Walking with God is a progressive journey. Every now and then you need to stop and look at where you are and realize how far the Lord has brought you. No matter how far you have come, you still have a long way to go. That is why none of us can talk about any of us because all of us are still being made.

36

While you may have victory in one area don't act like there isn't anything the devil could use to trip you up. He has your name, cell phone, and e-mail, and while you're trying to pretend to be deep, he has something or someone that will turn your world upside down. If it weren't for grace, you would have fallen and not gotten back up.

Paul reminds you that he had a life before Christ and he had to learn how to walk with God. It takes time to learn how to be spiritual. That is why every day of your life you need to surrender to the Holy Spirit to let Him work.

PRIOR PREPARATION EQUALS GOOD SUCCESS

Paul said we all have to experience the silent years, the period of prior preparation before our years of active service. God doesn't send you out until He makes you. He doesn't make you in the crowd. He makes you in the desert. That is what is wrong with a lot of saints today. They were made in the wrong place so they can't handle the promotions that come their way. They had no prior preparation before their time of active service.

The military calls this prior preparation basic training. Before they give soldiers a gun and put them on the battlefield, they go through basic training. Before they give them any type of promotion, they spend weeks breaking them down and preparing them to live in the worst situations so they can survive.

The Holy Ghost is your drill sergeant. He really doesn't care if you like Him. He is preparing you for the battle that is ahead so you will be able to stand when the enemy comes.

Paul said we all have silent years. If it was true for him, it is true for you. Let me remind you again that when God wants to make you, He does not rush the process.

IT'S TIME

There is no doubt that it is during the silent years that you will have your greatest growth spurt. You don't grow up on the mountain singing and shouting; you grow up in the desert. The purpose of God during this time is your making, and He does this best in the place of solitude.

Some of you may think you are spiritual adults, but you're still babies. Your greatest growth spurt will not happen in a crusade or a conference. Your greatest growth spurt occurs in the desert during times of sickness, failure, and disappointment. You don't know what life is until you've failed. You don't know what life is until you've been disappointed. You don't know what life is until you've been knocked down and almost knocked out. You don't truly know what life is until you've experienced failure, disappointment, disillusion, and hurt.

A great person is one who gets knocked down and allows God to stand them back up. A great person says, "I may have fallen, but my failure is not fatal or final because if God is for me, He is more than the world against me. If God is on my side, even though I fall seven times I will not be destroyed. Greater is He that's in me than he that's in the world." God takes you through the silent years to mature you. It is in those years that God gives you:

- Time to pray. Since God has you on hold, why not use this season to strengthen your prayer life.

- Time to think, study, and prepare. You have ample time to study and get ready for when God releases you.

- Time to listen. God will speak, and you need to open your ears to hear Him.

COMING ATTRACTIONS

It is in the silent years that you receive your first revelations.

<u>YOU GET A REVELATION OF GOD</u>

> *I want you to know, brothers, that the gospel
> I preached is not something that man made
> up. I did not receive it from any man, nor was
> I taught it; rather, I received it by revelation
> from Jesus Christ.* (Galatians 1:11-12)

Before God uses you, He will reveal Himself to you, because something is coming down the road that will make you question everything. In those moments you reach back for your first revelation of God.

When First Church was attempting to secure funding to purchase land and build, one of our sources turned us down. I began to question whether I had really heard from God, and if so, had I heard from Him correctly. One of the things I had to hold onto was the first revelation God gave me about who He is and what He could do. Before God shows you anything else He will show you Himself.

YOU GET A REVELATION OF YOURSELF

> *But when God, who set me apart from birth*
> *and called me by His grace, was pleased to*
> *reveal His Son in me so that I might preach*
> *Him among the Gentiles, I did not consult*
> *any man, nor did I go up to Jerusalem to see*
> *those who were apostles before I was, but I*
> *went immediately into Arabia and later re-*
> *turned to Damascus.* (Galatians 1:15-17)

God puts you in the desert to reveal the potential and propensity inside you to sin and mess up. Have you ever said, "I'd never do that!" and then found yourself doing exactly that? You don't know what you will do when your back is against the wall and the pressure is on. You don't know what you will do on a weak, bad, or a lonely day. If it weren't for the grace of God, you would be messing up every day. Thank God, His grace is sufficient.

God puts you in the desert by yourself with no one there to pat you on the back and tell you how great you are. You realize you are not a pretty sight. You see your issues. You see the sickness and perversion inside you. You wonder how God has put up with you as long as He has:

The Lord is compassionate and gracious, slow to anger, abounding in love. As a father has compassion on his children, so the Lord has compassion on those who fear Him; for He knows how we are formed, He rememb- ers that we are dust. (Psalm 103:8, 13-14)

YOU GET A REVELATION OF YOUR DESTINY AND PURPOSE

It is in the silent years that God shows you why you were born. Paul said the reason God put him in the desert, sent him to Arabia, put him on hold, and stuck him on the shelf was because He wanted to reveal Himself to Paul, He wanted to reveal Paul to himself, and He wanted to reveal Paul's purpose—to be a preacher to the Gentiles.

God wants to do the same things for you if you will let Him. God can't tell you what you need to know if you stay in the crowd. He walks up to you and says, "Come over here." You say, "Lord I've got my friends here," but God says, "If you come with me I will tell you something I won't tell anybody else. I have a purpose for you. I have a plan for you. I have destiny for you, but you have to come over here to get what I have for you."

Have you ever told God you would go where He is even though it's scary and uncertain? Since God has a plan for your life, then whatever He wants you to do is what you need to do. However He wants to use you, your heart should be saying Amen to His will.

Chapter Six
Faith to Endure

I WANT TO CONCLUDE this section on the silent years by looking at a man who spent one hundred and twenty years on one project. It didn't matter to him what others thought; he had been given an assignment and a promise from God and that was all he needed. When Noah said yes to God, he didn't know he would endure years of silence before it was all over.

DEFINING MOMENTS

Defining moments, according to Pastor Bill Hybels of Willow Creek Community Church in South Barrington, IL, are those moments which come our way that are pregnant with potential and power. If we seize them, they are moments that will change our lives forever. Usually when we speak of defining moments we are referring to a time or space where God is moving, changing, or making alterations in our lives. Those moments are defining, not because of what we do, but because God makes a move.

When God makes a move, nothing will ever be the same again.

In Genesis chapter six the defining moment is not a moment of action, but a moment of decision. The moment of decision is the defining moment and the action that follows is only the result of the decision. The defining moment is not when you do something; it is when you *decide* to do something. I pray I can get you to make a decision to change, stop or put an end to negative, destructive, sinful behavior. I pray I can get you to decide to change your lifestyle and start talking, acting, and thinking like what God says about you. I know your life would never be the same.

You need to get to a place where you decide that today is the last day you let anybody walk over you. You are somebody because God made you somebody. You have to start thinking, walking, talking, and acting like you are who God says you are. When you do that, take it from my personal experience, some people won't like it. Let me tell you a secret about human nature: Some people like it when you are broke down. There are some sick people who like you walking around with your face always tore up, sniffling, crying, and having fits. There are people who get off on your misery. They love feeling superior because you are always running to them with the broken pieces of your life, waiting for them to put it back together with their approval and acceptance. But the moment you decide to start walking with your head up instead of down; to start walking with confident strides instead of shuffling, to throw back your shoulders, stick out your chest and walk with dignity, somebody won't like it. So this is what you do: Look over your shoulder and wave goodbye!

THANK GOD FOR NOAH

Genesis chapter seven is when the flood takes place, but it is in chapter six that God makes the decision:

When men began to increase in number on the earth and daughters were born to them, the sons of God saw that the daughters of men were beautiful, and they married any of them they chose. Then the Lord said, "My Spirit will not contend with man forever, for he is mortal, his days will be a hundred and twenty years." The Nephilim were on the earth in those days—and also afterward— when the sons of God went to the daughters of men and had children by them. They were the heroes of old, men of renown. The Lord saw how great man's wickedness on the

47

earth had become and that every inclination of the thoughts of his heart was only evil all the time. The Lord was grieved that He had made man on the earth, and His heart was filled with pain. So the Lord said, "I will wipe mankind, whom I have created, from the face of the earth—men and animals, and creatures that move along the ground, and birds of the air—for I am grieved that I have made them." But Noah found favor in the eyes of the Lord. (Genesis 6:1-9)

The above passage tells us that humanity had reached an all time low and that wickedness and godlessness were the order of the day. The thoughts and deeds of men were evil all the time. God repents that He ever made man. It is as if God said to Himself, "I think I made a mistake. What was I thinking about the day that I made Adam? I was having a great time; I didn't have problems. I didn't have anybody rebelling or disobeying me. And I didn't have murder or rape." He was sorry that He ever made man and makes a decision to wipe man out. Not just man, but every animal, every bird, every bug, every lizard, every ant, and every grasshopper. God looked at the world, saw nothing but sin, disobedience, and rebellion and said, "I am sorry I ever made man. I am going to wipe man out."

"But Noah found favor in the eyes of God." In the midst of all that was going on, Noah was the exception, and he can teach you something about handling the period of inactivity called the silent years.

GOD SEES THOSE WHO ARE DIFFERENT

When God was looking down on the wickedness of His creation, in spite of all He saw wrong, He still saw Noah. Aren't you glad that when God looks on your job and see all those hellions, He can still see you? If I walk in a room with thirty people and twenty-nine of them are smoking, drinking, cussing, and acting crazy, I'm going to assume everybody in the room is smoking, drinking, cussing, and acting crazy. That is because I am human and limited. God is so much God that in a room of thirty people with twenty-nine acting crazy, He has such radar vision He can see the one who is different. God sees you surrounded by sin and trying to be different.

GOD IS WILLING TO USE THOSE WILLING TO BE DIFFERENT

God called Noah into service the moment He saw him and said, "Noah because you are different, I want to use you." Some of you may ask, "What's the use of being different?" I was listening to a sermon by Bishop Verone Ash and he said, "Some of you were okay until you started hanging around church folk." Bishop Ash is right. When you first got saved, you were in church every time the doors opened and tried to join every ministry. You were in the choir, on the usher board, and the greeting committee. But then you got around some of the ain'ts (not the saints) who said, "It don't take all that." You got around church people who have been saved just long enough to lose their joy, just long enough to be depressed, just long enough that nothing excites them anymore. They sit next to you and refuse to shout, clap their hands, or praise God. God says if you are willing to be different, He is willing to use you. God only uses people who are willing to pay the price.

GOD HONORS THOSE WHO WILL BECOME THE EXCEPTION

Noah found favor. That word *favor* means God blessed, honored, and elevated him. When God finds somebody who is willing to step out from the crowd and away from the pack, He uses and blesses them.

When the Lord first started using me, I was scheduled to preach at a large convention being held on the campus of Anderson University in Anderson, Indiana. A man was talking with a friend of mine and wondered how I had received this invitation since only a few preachers had the privilege. This man asked my friend if he knew me; my friend told him that he had known me since I was a child. The man asked my friend if I were an Anderson University alumnus and he said he didn't think so. The man asked, "Then how did he get on the program to preach?" and my friend responded, "Go ask him." The man never came to me, but I wish he would have. I would have told him it wasn't because I went to Anderson, had the right name, or the right pedigree. I was on the program because God put me there. God doesn't get any trouble out of me because I know where I have come from. I know I don't deserve to do great things for God. I know I don't have the right resume, pedigree, or background. There are a lot of people more qualified, competent, trained, and connected. I am being used because of God's favor.

If God is using you, there is no other way to explain it other than to call it God's favor. When the enemy would have destroyed you; when the devil would have wasted you, when your foes would have stomped you, God had favor. When they said you weren't going to make it; when they said you weren't going to be anything, when they said you would never succeed, God had favor.

You are trying to figure out how you have obtained all you have. Do you know there are people staying awake at night trying to figure that out, too? People watch you walk in church and their mind works overtime: "I don't understand it. How do they keep living, driving and dressing like they are? I would have thought by now they would have repossessed her house, car and clothes. How does she keep doing it? How does he keep landing on his feet?" I tell you how; it is God's favor. If God favors, blesses, and honors you, then it doesn't matter where you come from, who doesn't know you, who doesn't like you, or who doesn't support you. If the Lord is for you, no one can stand in your way.

GOD HAS BIG PLANS FOR YOU

No one likes the silent years. They are neither fun nor enjoyable, but they are necessary and productive. Let me just remind you that during your silent years others may not know your name or be acquainted with who you are, but God knows. You are precious to Him and He has BIG plans for you. That is why God is taking so long to make you. So settle down, your turn is coming!

PART TWO

THE SUFFERING YEARS

Chapter Seven
The Season of Suffering

SUFFERING IS A SUBJECT most of us don't like to discuss because no one willingly wants to suffer. But as you grow in the Lord, one of the things He allows is a season of suffering. Just like the painful, yet necessary, silent years where it seems like God has put you on hold and you're relegated to a period of inactivity, the suffering years are just as necessary if you're going to be what God wants and needs you to be.

After going through the silent years, the natural tendency is to feel that God is now ready to take the wraps off, put you on stage, introduce you to the world, and let you have a big debut. "Look out world, here I come. I've been silent, behind the scenes, and on the shelf. I know you've heard preaching, but you haven't heard me preach. I know you've heard praying, but you haven't heard me pray. I know you've heard teaching, but you haven't heard me teach. I know you've heard singing, but you haven't heard me sing." And just when you think God is getting ready to parade you onto the stage He says, "You are not quite done yet. Before I introduce you to the world, there us another season you have to go through and it is called the season of suffering."

The season of suffering is vital and necessary to your growth and development in the Lord. Somewhere I read that before God uses a man or woman greatly, He first of all hurts them deeply. God understands that unless you have gone through something, you will not be able to handle what is coming down the road. You're not going to be what God wants until you experience the season of suffering.

Chapter Eight
Just Another Ordinary Day

I WANT TO GIVE YOU an understanding of what God is doing when He allows, permits, or sends suffering into your life.

YOU CAN'T HAVE A TESTIMONY WITHOUT A TEST

Everyone who has made an impact in this world has known suffering at some level, so if you're going through a season of suffering you're in good company. Please don't try to judge life by where you are right now. If you're in a season of suffering, it's going to look like God is being unfair to you, but don't be deceived. When you get on the other side of suffering, you will discover that God was with you every step of the way.

A testimony is what God has brought you through. When you're going through, you don't need somebody with pious platitudes telling you a bunch of mumbo jumbo that makes no sense. When you're going through, you want somebody who can say, "Listen, I know what you're going through because I've been where you are, and the same God that brought me through is the same God that's able to bring you through." That is the power of a testimony.

If you never go through anything, you will never have a testimony of what God is able to do. If you want a great testimony, get ready for great suffering. You will never know God is a Healer until you get sick. You will never know God is a Provider until you get down to your last dime. You will never know God is a Waymaker until you are backed in a corner. You will never know that God will wipe tears from your eyes until you have cried all night long. You can't have a testimony without a test. Praise God, once you go through something no one can take your testimony away. You know that you know that you know the Lord brought you out! You don't want to be around somebody who has never gone through anything because they can't help you. A person who has never cried, failed, been hurt, or disappointed is not a very good counselor or comforter.

The Bible shows us that every person God used greatly went through suffering. The life of Joseph is a perfect example of this. When I look at the life of Joseph, I am always amazed at how God allowed him to go through suffering. One of the things that struck me about this story was how unfair Joseph's life seemed. He went through a lot of things he didn't deserve. If you stop reading before the end of the story you will get discouraged, but if you read to the end you will discover that God was with him all the way.

Genesis chapter thirty-seven reveals the events that would change Joseph's life in an unusual way. The day began like every other ordinary day; yet, before it's over nothing in Joseph's life would ever be the same. He woke up one bright, beautiful, God-kissed morning minding his own business. His father sent him to check on his brothers and he went thinking they would be glad to see him. He had no idea of their animosity toward him:

> *Now his brothers had gone to graze their father's flocks near Shechem, and Israel said to Joseph, "As you know, your brothers are grazing the flocks near Shechem. Come, I am going to send you to them." "Very well," he replied. So he said to him, "Go and see if all is well with your brothers and with the flocks, and bring word back to me." Then he sent him off from the Valley of Hebron. So Joseph went after his brothers and found them near Dothan. But they saw him in the distance, and before he reached them, they plotted to kill him. "Here comes that dreamer!" they*

said to each other. "Come now, let's kill him
and throw him into one of these cisterns and
say that a ferocious animal devoured him.
Then we'll see what comes of his dream."
(Genesis 37:12-15; 17-20)

Joseph's brothers saw him coming and the hatred and jealously they felt toward him boiled over. The first thing they wanted to do was kill him, but Reuben talked them out of that. They then decided to put him in a well and sell him to the Midianites, who sold him to the Ishmaelites, who sold him to the Egyptians. Joseph then began seventeen years of unbroken suffering.

Can you identify with Joseph? You wake up thinking it is going to be a good, yet ordinary, day and before the day is over all hell has broken loose. What makes me excited about this story—in spite of it being horrific, terrible, and ugly—is that when everybody else walked out, God walked in; when no one else was there, God was, and what no one else could do, God did!

IT'S HARD TO DROWN IN AN EMPTY WELL

Joseph's brothers put him in a well and sold him to the Midianites. You might not see it, but this is something to shout about. His brothers put him in a well, but guess what? The well was empty! There should have been water in the well and Joseph should have drowned, but God had fixed it so that the well was dry.

Joseph became the victim of his brothers' hatred. They put him in a pit and sold him as a slave. Joseph ended up in the house of Potiphar. You will see some horrific things happen to Joseph, but what I am about to share is really what is important, because the Lord was with Joseph.

There is only so much that people can do to hurt you. I'm glad that my life and destiny is not in the hands of people. What people mean for evil, God can turn around for good. People can put you in a pit, but they can't kill you. People can put you in a well, but they can't drown you. If God wants you to live, there is nothing anyone can do about it. If God has a plan and purpose for your life—and believe me He does—you can't die until you fulfill it.

How many times have you been dropped in a well without any water in it? How many times have people put you down and thought they had destroyed you? With God on your side it doesn't matter who is against you. People can be vicious, but God is still in control.

There may be some ugly and painful things that are going to happen to you, but remember that the Lord is with you and that is what matters most. You think that what matters is who is on your side, how much money is in the bank, who your friends are, who you know, and who you are connected to. But none of that matters. If everybody else turns against you and the Lord is with you that is more than enough to make it no matter what is going on in your life. God with you is more than the whole world against you.

NEXT STOP: DESTINY

Being dropped in an empty well is something worth shouting about. But guess what? This story gets even better. Joseph's brothers sold him to the Midianites, who sold him to the Ishmaelites, who sold him to Potiphar who happened to live in Egypt. In the well, out the well; out of the well to the Midianites; from the Midianites to the Ishmaelites; from the Ishmaelites to Potiphar to Egypt.

The reason I'm excited isn't because they were dragging him around from city to city; Joseph's destiny was not in the well, with the Midianites or the Ishmaelites. His destiny was in Egypt, so every move took him closer to his destiny! Even though it looked like the pathway to destiny wasn't clear, God knew who and what to use to get Joseph to where He wanted him to be.

Some of you are in places where you're still trying to figure out how or why you're there. The reason you're there is because God is taking you someplace. Every move you make, every city you go to, every job you have, every career move is taking you one step closer to your destiny.

You may be in the well, but you're not going to stay there. You can rest in the well because there is no water in it. You're not going to die. You're out of the well, but with the Midianites and that's okay. Just ride in the wagon as far as the Midianites will take you. The Midianites sold you to the Ishmaelites. That's okay, too. Just hang with the Ishmaelites as long as they will have you. When they don't want you anymore and they sell you to Potiphar, don't get bent out of shape. Potiphar's house is where God wants you to be.

FEAR, FRUSTRATION, AND FAITH

What must Joseph have gone through? I never read this story without my heart breaking. For a moment imagine yourself in Joseph's place in the well. Can't you hear him yelling at his brothers, "Reuben? Simeon? All right now, y'all stop playing. It's dark down here. I'm telling daddy. This ain't funny. Get me out of here!" Let me show you how mean and evil people can be:

As they sat down to eat their meal, they looked up and saw a caravan of Ishmaelites coming from Gilead. Their camels were loaded with spices, balm and myrrh, and they were on their way to take them down to Egypt. Judah said to his brothers, "What will we gain if we kill our brother and cover up his blood? Come, let's sell him to the Ishmaelites and not lay our hands on him; after all, he is our brother, our own flesh and blood." His brothers agreed. So when the Midianite merchants came by, his brothers pulled Joseph up out of the cistern and sold him for twenty shekels of silver to the Ishmaelites, who took him to Egypt. (Genesis 37:25-28)

Can you imagine what was going through Joseph's mind sitting in the wagon, watching his brothers fade in the distance knowing they had just sold him into slavery? What was he thinking? How did his heart feel? What emotions coursed through him? I think they're the same emotions and feelings you have when entering the season of suffering.

FEAR

I know saints don't believe they should fear, but if you are honest, you will admit that when you initially hit the season of suffering the first natural response is fear. When the doctor says its cancer, you experience fear. Praise may come later, but the first response is fear. If you get a pink slip, your first response is not to speak in tongues. You may want to speak, but it isn't in tongues! The fear covers three areas:

- The present: "What's going on with me?" "Why is this happening to me?"

- The future: "What's going to happen to me?" "How am I going to make it?" "How am I going to handle this?"

- Other people's response: "How will people treat me now that this has happened?"

Suffering produces fear. It's okay to be saved, sanctified, filled with the Holy Ghost, and still experience fear. I know the Bible says, *"God has not given us the spirit of fear"* (2 Timothy 1:7) and that is true. As a believer you don't have the spirit of fear, which means you don't live in fear and it doesn't control your life. It doesn't mean you're never afraid. *"What times I am afraid, I will trust in the Lord"* (Psalm 56:3). David said there are times he gets afraid. Aren't there times you get afraid? When those times happen, you don't give into the fear and let a spirit of fear overtake you. When you are afraid, lean on the Lord: *"I will lift up my eyes to the hills—where does my help come from? My help comes from the Lord, the Maker of heaven and earth"* (Psalm 121:1-2). When afraid, trust in the Lord.

Don't let anybody tell you that when bad news comes or you go through suffering you shouldn't be afraid. You don't have a spirit of fear, but your first human response is fear. Then faith kicks in and you say, "God, I don't know what's going to happen, but I'm going to put my faith in you."

FRUSTRATION

I keep seeing Joseph in the well, yelling, and calling for his brothers to get him out. I keep seeing Joseph sitting in that caravan, hands and feet tied, a slave of the Midianites wondering, "How in the world did I get here? I woke up this morning and did what daddy asked and here I am with a bunch of strangers, sold by my own brothers."

Suffering is frustrating especially when you feel it's undeserved. Sometimes you don't understand what is going on and why things are happening. You pay your tithes, go to church, and try to live right. "Why me? Why now?" Isn't that what you ask?

When you're suffering, you feel powerless. Have you ever looked at things and thought, "I'm an intelligent person, I've got pretty good strength. I have good business savvy. I've got pretty good mental comprehension. I've always been able to fix everything else, so why can't I fix this?" Is there something in your life you can't fix? Doesn't it make you feel powerless? People going through divorce often feel this way. They may handle problems all day, so why can't they fix their marriage? They counsel and solve other people's problems, so why can't they fix this? They're a prayer warrior and intercessor, so why is their world falling apart? When you're going through suffering, you feel frustrated because you feel powerless.

You also feel helpless. Several years ago I was sick and literally flat on my back and could do nothing for myself. I discovered then that being helpless and dependent on somebody else for everything was no fun. When you are going through suffering, you feel helpless, inept, puny, and weak. You are like a little baby. Sometimes you start crying and you don't know why. You look around and your world is spiraling out of control and everything is spinning so fast. You want to grab something to hold onto and you can't. You feel helpless and that is frustrating.

You also feel vulnerable. There is nothing worse than feeling like you can't defend yourself. Have you ever been lied on? You want to run to everybody who heard it and say, "IT'S NOT TRUE!" The only problem is you don't know who heard it. You want to take ads out in the media saying, "I DIDN'T DO IT!" and you feel vulnerable.

FAITH

At some point, if handled correctly, suffering leads to faith. It is hard to believe, but if you have ever been through a season of suffering, you know I'm right.

When you're suffering, God strips you of everything and everybody. It is not suffering as long as you have a roomful of people around you. As long as you have people cheering you on and patting you on the back, you're not suffering. You aren't suffering until God strips you of everything and everybody: your money, job, health, and self-confidence.

The devil believes that by pushing you he will eventually push you off a cliff into the abyss. The devil is crazy. He doesn't realize that he is pushing you back to your place of original strength. That is why suffering is good because it pushes you back to God. You don't lean on your friends, job, money, or education. Suffering pushes you back to God where He is the only one you have: His promises, presence, power, and peace. You learn how to lean and depend on Him. If not for the Lord, you won't make it. He alone is able to hold, help, and strengthen you. He is able to do what needs to be done:

> *To Him who is able to keep you from falling and to present you before His glorious presence without fault and with great joy—to the only God our Savior be glory, majesty, power and authority, through Jesus Christ our Lord, before all ages, now and forever more! Amen.* (Jude 24)

During the season of suffering you will be afraid, but trust in the Lord. You will be frustrated, but know that God is working in your life. And if you handle the season of suffering right, it will increase your faith, because it pushes you back to God.

TROUBLES DON'T LAST ALWAYS

Your suffering is never just about you; God always has something bigger in mind. God was behind everything that was going on in Joseph's life and was working for the good of Joseph and a nation. God knew where Joseph was going and what he would need. He used everything in Joseph's life to bring him to where He needed him to be. If you would take a page out of Joseph's life, you would learn three powerful truths about trouble:

YOUR TROUBLES ARE TIMED

The old people said "Troubles don't last always," and they were absolutely right. When you are going through, it seems like trouble will last forever. You need to remember that your troubles have a beginning and an end. God knows how much you can bear. There is coming a day when God is going to put an end to the troubles in your life.

YOUR TROUBLES HAVE A PURPOSE

You are not going through just to be going through. There is something that God is doing in the process of your suffering. He may be doing something in, to, or with you. There is always a purpose for suffering. If you are in a place of suffering, you need to know that God has a purpose for it.

YOUR TROUBLES ARE REWARDED

God knows what you're going through. If you go through suffering with the right attitude, God is going to pay you back. You might not believe it right now, but God is keeping a record of everything. Today some of you are in a place of blessing, enlargement, or prosperity and you can look back and realize that where you are now is directly related to where you have been. God is blessing you now because you kept your attitude right while going through. You kept serving, praising, and loving God when you were going through suffering. He has now brought you to a place where the trouble is over and He is blessing you. The Psalmist understood suffering well: *"Weeping may endure for the night, but joy comes in the morning"* (Psalm 30:5).

Chapter Nine
God Will Prosper You

GENESIS 39:2 SAYS, *"THE Lord was with Joseph and he prospered."* Wait a minute! Joseph was a slave in a foreign land so what is this prospering stuff? How does a resume that reads slave, foreigner, abandoned by brothers, dropped in a pit, and sold into slavery become prosperous? The Lord was with Joseph. When the Lord is with you, He makes things happen that would not ordinarily happen, and He does what no one else can do. So how did Joseph prosper?

<u>JOSEPH WAS FAITHFUL</u>

I wish I could meet with you one-on-one and tell you that if you want to be anything in life, you have to start by being faithful. Forget your illusions (or delusions) of grandeur about how you want God to use you if you're not faithful. God doesn't use anybody that is not faithful. If you're going to be used by God, you start by being faithful. Joseph was a slave who didn't have anything of his own and yet was faithful over the stuff that belonged to his master.

Until you can be faithful over what belongs to another person, God will never bless you with something of your own. Some of you want to have a ministry; you can forget about a ministry until you can help somebody in their ministry. Some of you want to do something great; God says if you want to do something great, first work behind the scenes to make someone else look good. When He sees you being faithful, He will reward you. Jesus says in the last days God is going to separate the sheep from the goats, and He will determine who will go where based on their faithfulness.

JOSEPH WAS FOCUSED

Joseph kept his heart and mind on his dream. Joseph had a dream before he left home and even in Egypt he stayed focused. Even while helping Potiphar he didn't let go of his dream. He learned how to put his dream on hold to make Potiphar's dream come true.

You should buy the book *Free to Dream: Discover Your Divine Destiny* by Bishop Charles E. Blake. Bishop Blake says that it is only when you can keep your dream alive when no one else believes in it that your dream will come true. If your dream can't survive people attacking it, it's not from God. If you wilt and die because someone laughed at your dream, it will never come true. If you can stand people laughing at your dream and hold onto it anyhow, you will be amazed how God will make your dream come true.

JOSEPH WAS FAVORED

When you read the story of Joseph, you will discover that his father gave him a coat and his brothers hated him for it:

> *Now Israel loved Joseph more than any of his other sons, because he had been born to him in his old age; and he made a richly orna-mented robe for him. When his brothers saw that their father loved him more than any of them, they hated him and could not speak a kind word to him.* (Genesis 37:3-4)

They eventually took the coat, dipped it in blood, and told their father that a wild beast had devoured him:

> *Here comes that dreamer!" they said to each other. "Come now, let's kill him and throw him into one of these cisterns and say that a*

ferocious animal devoured him. Then we'll see what comes of his dreams. (Genesis 37:19-20)

Even in the place of Joseph's affliction, God blessed him and caused him to prosper. This is where the story of Joseph shows the reality of the Bible. Having gone through and survived what his brothers did to him—to still excel and achieve in spite of it—one would think his days of suffering would be behind him. Not so. Genesis chapter thirty-nine shows that Joseph is about to endure more suffering at the hands of Mrs. Potiphar:

One day he went into the house to attend to his duties and none of the household servants was inside. She caught him by his cloak and said, "Come to bed with me!" But he left his cloak in her hand and ran out of the house. When she saw that he had left his cloak in her hand and had run out of the house, she called her household servants. "Look," she said to them, "this Hebrew has been brought to us to make sport of us! He came in here to sleep with me, but I screamed. When he heard me scream for help, he left his cloak beside me and ran out of the house." She kept his cloak beside her until his master came home. Then she told him this story. (Genesis 39:11-17)

People think your power is in your coat and lay awake at night plotting and planning how to take it from you. Joseph understood that the coat could be taken, but the power was in God's favor. You can take a person's position and they will still be anointed. Favor is not in a job, position, or title. Favor is inside you. Joseph was in Egypt, but he prospered because of favor.

Joseph became the object of Mrs. Potiphar's attention. Although he refused her advances, Joseph had to again suffer for something he didn't do. He suffered false accusations when Mrs. Potiphar lied on him. He suffered false punishment when Potiphar threw him in prison. He suffered false friends when he interpreted a dream and the cupbearer forgot all about him. It seemed as if Joseph's life had gone from bad to worse. Ever been there?

So what is the purpose of suffering, especially when it seems we don't deserve it?

SUFFERING TRIES US

"He knows the way that I take; when he has tried me, I will come forth as gold" (Job 23:10). Gold is one of the hardest objects in the world. When first mined, it is encased or covered with impurities. Gold is put in a furnace to burn away the impurities so that the pureness can come forth.

You need to understand that when God allows suffering it is not intended to kill you, but to make you. The fire is used to burn up everything that is not going to bring Him glory. The furnace burns off the attitudes, spirits, thoughts, desires, and mindsets you shouldn't have. The fire is getting rid of everything (and everyone) you are going to leave in the furnace. When you come out you will be like gold—stronger, better, purer, and ready to be used. You can't come out until you have gone through the fire.

Suffering tries you because some of you don't have anything but a good shout. The minute something doesn't go your way you want to curse both God and the saints! God puts you in the furnace so the stuff He can't and won't use gets burnt off. Don't ever worry about the stuff left in the furnace, because what is left are impurities and dross that you needed to get rid of it anyway.

SUFFERING TRAINS US

Suffering trains you for what is coming. No pain, no gain. No cross, no crown. The writer of Hebrews said:

> *No discipline (suffering) seems pleasant at the time, but painful. Later on, however, it produces a harvest of righteousness and peace for those who have been trained by it.* (Hebrews 12:11)

Athletes don't wait until an Olympic year to start training. They are running, lifting weights, exercising, and working out now for something that is going to occur in the future. Training isn't fun or necessarily enjoyable, but when they get to the Olympics they want to be able to compete for a prize.

What I am trying to tell you is that God is trying to take you somewhere. God is training you now so that when you get to where you are going, you will be able to stand and win the victory. Nothing trains you like suffering.

SUFFERING TEMPERS US

You ask, "Why am I suffering?" The answer is: God wants to temper you. When you read the story of Joseph's life, you discover he was a child of privilege and position and his father's favorite. God had a plan for Joseph, and He knew that in order for Joseph to handle what He had for him He had to temper him. What his brothers did was terrible, but God used it to make him. What Mrs. Potiphar did was terrible, but God used it to make him. After being put in the well, sold into slavery, and thrown into jail, all the starch was out of Joseph. The suffering tempered him so that he could handle promotion.

God has big plans for some of you, but you're too full of yourself. God is going to have to humble you a little bit because you are too impressed with yourself. He will take you through suffering so you'll recognize that if it weren't for the Lord you wouldn't be where you are. All of the glory goes to God. Suffering brings you to a place where you realize if the Lord doesn't help, there won't be any help. If you humble yourself, God will exalt you in due time. If you humble yourself, the Lord will use you. If you humble yourself, God will bless you. God only blesses people He knows He can trust.

PART THREE

THE PURPOSE FOR THE PAIN

Chapter Ten
The Purpose for the Pain

THOSE SILENT YEARS (WHEN it seems like God has you on hold), and the suffering years (when it looks like God is breaking you), are two painful periods to experience.

When going through the years of silence or suffering, you might experience emotional pain. It is almost as if the enemy attacks your mind. Before something happens in your flesh it takes root in your mind. If you don't think it, you will never do it. If you can handle your mind, you can deal with your flesh. There is also spiritual pain when it seems as if you can't get your groove on. Everybody around you is shouting, but you can't work up a shout. Everybody around you is praising God, and you're sitting like a bump on a log. It's not that you don't want to praise God or don't have a reason to praise Him, but sometimes life will bring you to a place where you don't feel like praising Him. One of the things you must confess is that the seasons of silence and suffering are very painful periods.

During the silent and suffering years you feel forgotten, neglected, overlooked, and in some ways unneeded. And if you're not careful, you will begin to question your value and worth. The Church has put emphasis on what you "do" which makes you feel like you only have value as long as you're doing something. Your value to God is never connected to what you do. The old saints told me:

> *For it is by grace you have been saved,*
> *through faith— and this not from yourselves,*
> *it is the gift of God— not by works, so that no*
> *one can boast.* (Ephesians 2:8-9)

They quoted it, but they didn't live it. Most churches have an unwritten doctrine of a works theology and will tell you that the way to prove your love for God is to get busy; the busier you are the more love you must have. After forty years of leading God's people, I have concluded that isn't true. Some of the busiest people in the church are also the most neurotic, needy, and messed up because they're looking for a job or title to validate them. Unfortunately, they don't understand that if they're not anything without a title, they won't be anything with one.

God doesn't love you because of what you do. He loves you because of who you are. There is nothing you can do to make God love you more than He already does.

You may not believe that because you live in a world where people love you based on what you do for them. The moment you can't do anything for them is the moment they will put you down. But, the way people treat you is not the way God treats you. He loves you no matter what. You cannot earn the love of God; you only need to learn how to accept the love He has for you.

God didn't wait for you to get yourself together before He started loving you. When you were on your way to hell, God still loved you. He can never love you more than He already does. The Word of God says:

Very rarely will anyone die for a righteous man, though for a good man some might possibly dare to die. But God demonstrates His own love for us in this: While we were still sinners, Christ died for us. (Romans 5:7-8)

When you're going through the silent and suffering years, the temptation is to feel like you don't have value or worth. If you're not careful and prayerful, the silent and suffering years will cause you to doubt your value, worth, and God's love. That is a very painful experience.

When you're going through these years, everything hurts—your mind, body, and spirit. Suffering is always painful and it can make you bitter, resentful, and hardened to the things of God. That is why it is so important to understand what God is up to when He allows suffering and pain in your life.

A MAN NAMED JOB

You wouldn't mind going through seasons of pain and suffering if you knew there was a reason or a purpose for what is happening in your life. We often talk about the purpose and plan of God. Usually what we mean is that God has a plan for our lives relative to who we're going to marry, where we will live, what our life's work will be, where we will go to college, and so on. God is concerned about all of that, but God also has a purpose and a plan for the seasons and period of our lives relative to what we will experience and go through. Within that plan is some pain and suffering. We don't want to hear that the pain comes from God and that it has a purpose, but it is true:

> *In the land of Uz there lived a man whose name was Job. This man was blameless and upright; he feared God and shunned evil. He had seven sons and three daughters, and he owned seven thousand sheep, three thou-*

sand camels, five hundred yoke of oxen and five hundred donkeys, and had a large number of servants. He was the greatest man among all the people of the East. His sons used to take turns holding feasts in their homes, and they would invite their three sisters to eat and drink with them. When a period of feasting had run its course, Job would send and have them purified. Early in the morning he would sacrifice a burnt offering for each of them, thinking, "Perhaps my children have sinned and cursed God in their hearts." This was Job's regular custom. (Job 1:1-5)

Job was living the life that we are often told every child of God should and can have: blameless, upright, blessed, and prosperous. If you just read Job 1:1-5, you will get a perverted view of life if you think that salvation prevents problems. That is not what the Word of God teaches. Job's story shows that material wealth is not the only barometer of God's blessings. I believe God wants you to be blessed and prosperous. I believe God wants to give increase in your life. I believe God honors seed that is sown and He will produce a harvest.

Yet, there is another side to the story. Just having blessings, getting a new car, a new house, or getting a promotion is not the only barometers of the favor of God in your life. If you build your life around stuff, what are you going to do when it's gone? You must have something that is bigger, stronger, and more lasting than anything else. God wants you to have a meaningful relationship with Him, so that when material things are gone you still have a relationship that is real, vital, strong, and vibrant. There is more to God's blessings than just things. Sometimes saints get it backwards; we get stuff and then want to serve God. We are to come to God who has everything and whatever we need, He will supply.

God sends blessings *and* burdens and both are gifts. You think everything good comes from God and everything bad comes from the devil, so at the first bump in the road you want to rebuke the devil. Everything in life that hurts is not from the devil.

Have you ever gone through something that made you wonder, "What is God up to?" If you have, then the story of Job was written especially for you. Chapter one opens with Job being the richest man in the east; perfect and upright. He was a man who walked with God and served Him. The word *perfect* doesn't mean he was without fault, it means he was whole and balanced.

This good man was about to suffer for something he didn't do. Job becomes the epitome of suffering and it's only through the suffering that he really comes to know God. God permitted the pain because Job was going to learn something about God in pain that he could never learn in pleasure. It is the painful places of life that allows you to know God. It is when you are backed into a corner and everything that can go wrong does go wrong that you learn about God.

In chapter one Job's life reads and sounds so much like our own which is why so many of us have been able to relate to him. Job woke up one morning with no idea that before the day ended his whole world would have changed. He had no idea that his whole life would be turned upside down and inside out. Job didn't know that God and Satan had been discussing him and that God had taken Satan's challenge, and in essence, staked His reputation on Job. Job had no idea that God would allow Satan to unleash an attack on him that would send his world reeling. Job didn't know that he was the central character in a divine drama and that by the time it was all over he would have learned lessons about God that would instruct every generation that followed on the ways of God.

WHERE IS GOD?

One of the things that make the Book of Job so compelling is the honesty. Here was a man going through and he wanted to know why. God seemed absent and Job said, "I've looked everywhere for Him, but I can't find Him."

> *Even today my complaint is bitter; his hand is heavy in spite of my groaning. If only I knew where to find Him; if only I could go to his dwelling! I would state my case before Him and fill my mouth with arguments. I would find out what He would answer me, and consider what He would say. Would He oppose me with great power? No, He would not press charges against me. There an upright man could present his case before Him, and I would be delivered forever from my judge. But if I go to the east, He is not there; if I go to the west, I do not find Him. When He is at work in the north, I do not see Him; when He turns to the south, I catch no glimpse of Him.*
> (Job 23:1-9)

Have you ever looked for God and couldn't find Him? Have you ever read the Bible and it was just dry words?

Have you ever tried to pray and your prayer hit the ceiling, dropped down, and hit you on the head? Have you ever tried to work up a song and the words wouldn't come? Have you ever tried to dance and you tripped over your own two feet? You looked for God and He was nowhere to be found and like Job you wanted to shout, "I wish I knew where to find Him!"

God is always with you even when you can't sense Him: *"But he knows the way that I take"* (Job 23:10). You are not out of God's sight or vision; you can't find Him, but He can find you. You are never lost to Him. The joy of the believer is that He knows what you're going through and how much you can bear.

THE WISDOM OF GOD

I know that you can do all things; no plan of yours can be thwarted. You asked, "Who is this that obscures my counsel without know-ledge?" Surely I spoke of things I did not un-derstand, things too wonderful for me to know. You said, "Listen now, and I will speak; I will question you, and you shall answer me." My ears had heard of you but now my eyes have seen you. (Job 42:1-5)

91

Job thought he knew God before, but after going through suffering he received a new revelation. In the end Job looked back on his pain and realized that God was far wiser than he was. God knows what He is doing and He has a purpose and a plan for all that is happening:

- The first thing the wisdom of God takes into account is *what*. God looks at you and decides what He is going to let the devil hit you with.

- The second thing God allows is the timing of *when* the devil can implement the what.

- The third thing is *who*. God sends certain things, to certain people, at certain times.

There are things that are happening today because that is the what; the time is now because this is the when and you're the who, because God knows that you can handle it. When you wonder, "Why is this happening now?" it is happening now because you can handle it now. It would have killed you before. If it is happening now, this is the best time. What you know today is that now you can handle it because God wouldn't have sent it until the time was right. His wisdom looks at what, when, and who. It's all part of His plan.

THE FAITHFULNESS OF GOD

Not only did Job learn about the presence and wisdom of God, but he also learned about the faithfulness of God. God was with him and was taking care of him. You look at all that Job went through, or what you or a loved one is going through, and think how unfair life is. There are three things to remember about the faithfulness of God:

GOD LIMITED SATAN

The devil wanted to wipe Job out and God said no; he could test Job, but he couldn't lay his hand on Job's life. God drew a line and told Satan he could only go so far and if he crossed it, he would have to answer to Him. The devil left the presence of God. He didn't try to negotiate because he understood that he was no match for God. Even though you don't see it in your life, God has drawn a line between you and the devil and has said that is as far as he can go.

GOD SUSTAINED JOB

Why didn't Job crack up? He lost his children, his health, and his possessions, so why didn't he lose his mind? Because God is faithful and even in our worst moments He is sustaining and keeping us alive. You may be weak, feeble, and feel like you can't go any further, but the fact that you are alive is testimony to the grace and faithfulness of God. You ought to be happy that God is keeping you alive. You haven't lost your mind because God is sustaining you. You are still standing with your joy, praise, and peace because God is keeping you. He is faithful.

GOD REWARDED JOB

The story of Job ends with him getting twice as much as he had before:

> *After Job had prayed for his friends, the Lord made him prosperous again and gave him twice as much as he had before. All his brothers and sisters and everyone who had known him before came and ate with him in his house. They comforted and consoled him over all the trouble the Lord had brought*

upon him, and each one gave him a piece of silver and a gold ring. The Lord blessed the latter part of Job's life more than the first. (Job 42:10-12)

While in the suffering season, don't become bitter, mad, or develop a bad attitude. Keep on praising, shouting, trusting, and serving God and He will give you double for your trouble.

Chapter Eleven
In the Hands of the Master Potter

GOD EXEMPTS NO ONE from the seasons of life. If you think that God is so impressed with you that He is going to give you a free pass, you have another thought coming. You want to believe that if you pray hard enough, fast long enough, and shout loud enough that you will make or convince God to let you slide. God is not that impressed with you. If God made Moses, Abraham, David, and everybody else go through seasons, then who do you think you are that He is not going to put you through, too? Everybody that God used He took through the seasons of life. Paul, the greatest figure in the Christian faith apart from Jesus, went through a season of silence and suffering. Jesus went through the same seasons. You might as well get ready for your turn.

Those with the greatest testimonies endure the greatest suffering. Some people want to go to bed a blunder and wake up a wonder. Some people want to get saved today, receive the Holy Ghost tonight, and be a miracle worker tomorrow. Some people want instant, overnight success. It doesn't happen. If you want a testimony, you have to go through a test. A testimony is a report of what God has brought you through. If He hasn't brought you through anything, you don't have anything to report. The greater the suffering, the greater the testimony.

When God wants to make a person, He starts by breaking them. If you haven't been broken, you are not going to be great.

I heard a preacher tell a story about Dr. Gardner Calvin Taylor. A friend knew that Dr. Taylor loved classical music and invited him to hear a young concert pianist and contralto singer. The person who invited him raved about how great this singer was. After the concert was over his friend asked him, "Wasn't she great?" Dr. Taylor said, "She was very good." His friend was insulted because he thought she was fantastic. Dr. Taylor said, "She was very good." His friend said, "She was great!" Dr. Taylor said, "She was very good, and one day she will be great. She's a good singer now, but when life hurts her, she will be a great singer."

There is something about being broken that lets the best part come forth. A rose doesn't release its fragrance until it is broken. Grapes become wine after they are broken. Greatness comes out after a person has been broken. If God is going to make you, He will start by breaking you. You don't like it, but it's true and it's still

God's method: He takes you down before He lifts you up. He empties you before He fills you. He breaks you before He makes you. He lets you die before He raises you up. You will never have Easter without Good Friday. There has to be blood, pain, suffering, and death. After Friday comes Sunday, and when Sunday comes nothing can hold you back.

We looked at the life of Paul in a previous chapter and discovered the purpose for his pain was not just to teach him something about God, but also to teach him something about himself. Most of us are familiar with his story, how before his conversion he was an enemy of the church and one day on the road to Damascus, armed with papers permitting him to destroy the church, he was converted. Paul, then named Saul, met Jesus Christ and his life was never the same. God used this man to become one of the prominent New Testament figures in the early church:

> *I know a man in Christ who fourteen years ago was caught up to the third heaven. Whether it was in the body or out of the body I do not know—God knows. And I know that this man—whether in the body or apart from the body I do not know, but God know—was caught up to paradise. He heard inex-*

pressible things; things that man is not permitted to tell. I will boast about a man like that, but I will not boast about myself, except about my weaknesses. Even if I should choose to boast, I would not be a fool, because I would be speaking the truth. But I refrain, so no one will think more of me than is warranted by what I do or say. To keep me from becoming conceited because of these surpassingly great revelations, there was given me a thorn in my flesh, a messenger of Satan, to torment me. Three times I pleaded with the Lord to take it away from me. But He said to me, "My grace is sufficient for you, for my power is made perfect in weakness." Therefore I will boast all the more gladly about my weaknesses, so that Christ's power may rest on me. (2 Corinthians 12:2-9)

We know about Paul's thorn in the flesh and how he prayed three times to have it removed. I have concluded there are some valuable lessons God taught Paul out of his pain, and they are the same lessons God wants to teach us.

STAY HUMBLE

The purpose for the pain was to teach Paul how to handle blessings. Second Corinthians 12:2-9 can only be understood and appreciated in connection with Second Corinthians chapters ten and eleven. That is where Paul defended his apostleship against people questioning his authenticity. They remembered his past reputation and felt that he should just be glad they let him in the church. Some of those people's cousins are still around today. God sends sinners to church, saves them, fills them, anoints them, and some people wonder, "Who do they think they are?" Well, they're a blood-washed child of God just like you with all the rights and privileges of any other child of God. Just because a person has a past is no reason for you to turn your nose up or thumb down. As quiet as it's kept, you have a past, too.

One of the things that God hates is pride, a haughty spirit or a proud look while a humble spirit is God's delight. Most times when God greatly blesses someone, He sends along some pain. The pain is to teach the person how to humbly accept the blessings of God. He has given me the privilege and pleasure of rubbing shoulders with many of the great people of God who have something in their life that keeps them humble. You see their public persona, but there is some besetting sin, some weakness, some physical malady, some event in their past that keeps them humble before God. While you're caught up in the public revelation, you don't see the private pain that keeps them balanced as they handle the blessings that God has put on them.

God is a jealous God and He will not share His glory with anyone. When you get beside yourself and start thinking that you're God, He will slap you down, move you out of the way, and use somebody else. Because He wants to keep using you, He puts some pain in your life, a thorn in the flesh, some struggle that keeps you from getting the big head. Every time you would start to act crazy, God reminds you there are things you're still dealing with and you become more humble. Humbleness helps you handle what God has for you. God gives you pain to teach you how to humbly accept the blessings of God. Truly great people know that all they have comes from God. The first purpose for your pain is to prepare you for blessings, but you must be humble when they come.

JUST SAY YES

Paul's thorn was also used to teach him how to submit to God's will. Paul said he sought the Lord three times to remove the thorn. God permitted the pain in Paul's life so he would learn how to say yes. You wonder about the purpose for the pain in your life. One purpose is to bring you to a place of surrender where you learn how to say yes. Paul prayed three times for God to take the thorn away and God finally said, "I am not moving it." Paul had to come to a place of surrender and acceptance where it wasn't his will, but God's will.

One way God will do this is through failure. Failure is the back door to more than success. Sometimes failure is the back door to blessing. Sometimes failure is a set up. Sometimes God let's you fail to give you what He had for you all the time. Sometimes God will let you fail because He has something bigger down the road. He knows if you succeed at a lower level you will be content and never reach for what is ahead:

> *When He had finished speaking, He said to Simon, "Put out into deep water, and let down the nets for a catch." Simon answered, "Master we've worked hard all night and haven't caught anything. But because you say so, I will let down the nets." When they had done so, they caught such a large number of fish that their nets began to break. So they signaled their partners in the other boat to come and help them, and they came and*

filled both boats so full that they began to sink. (Luke 5:4-7)

Peter had toiled all night fishing and had caught nothing. It wasn't until Peter failed at what he was doing, that God opened up a blessing that he couldn't handle. You need to learn how to say, *"Nevertheless, not my will, but thy will be done."*

There are some things that will only happen when you learn how to say yes. Worrying about your marriage? God is waiting on you to say yes, and the minute you do, He can and will handle your marriage. Figuring out how to pay your bills? God is waiting on you to say yes, and the minute you do, He will bless your money. Trying to figure out how to handle the disease in your body? God is waiting on you to say yes, and the minute you do, He is a healer. There are some things that won't change until you say yes, and the minute you do God starts working, moving, acting, to change situations and circumstances. There is power in the yes.

LEAN ON GOD

The purpose for the pain is to teach you to rely on God. Paul sought the Lord three times to remove the thorn, but the reply from God was that His grace was sufficient for him.

Sometimes you rely on all the wrong things— money, friends, connections, education, and ability—but life will bring you to a place where the only One you can rely on is God. You can have all of the money in the world, but money doesn't cure cancer. You can have all of the money in the world, but money won't give you a good night's sleep. You can have all of the money in the world, but money won't buy a real friend. Life will bring you to a place where all you have is God, and in that moment you will discover that you can rely on Him. You can't rely on people because the arm of flesh will fail you, but the Lord will never let you down.

Paul prayed three times and God answered, "*My grace is sufficient for you, for my power is made perfect in weakness.*" Paul decided to give God his weakness and take on His strength. God's strength is greater than any other strength in the world. If you are going to count on somebody, why not count on God?

Since His grace is sufficient, He is able to bring you out more than a conqueror. If you wonder whether or not He has the power to do it, you are talking about the One whose power made this world, created man-kind, sustains the universe, got Jesus out of the grave, saved your soul, washed your sins away, and all power is in His hand. He is God all by Himself:

> *Now to Him who is able to do exceedingly abundantly above all that we ask or think, according to the power that works in us, to Him be glory in the church by Christ Jesus to all generations, forever and ever. Amen.* (Ephesians 3:20-21, NKJV)

Chapter Twelve
The Seasons of Live

THE WHOLE PREMISE OF making the most of your time is to help you understand that all of us have been given a certain amount of time:

> *The length of our days is seventy years or eighty, if we have the strength; yet their span is but trouble and sorrow, for they quickly pass, and we fly away.* (Psalm 90:10)

The bottom line is that you have not come into this world to stay. When I was growing up, we used to say there were only two things in life you could be sure of: death and taxes, but I have lived long enough to discover that if you have the right accountant, you can even avoid taxes.

It doesn't matter who you are, what you have, or where you live, all of us are here for a time or season. None of us have come here to stay. I'm trying to get you to understand that in the framework of time you have left you must ask God to help you make the most of it. You have to maximize the time that God has given you.

You can't afford to waste or squander it. You must ask God for wisdom to make the most of your time.

One of the ways you will do that is to understand that the time you have is broken down into seasons. Life is not an unbroken continuum. There are seasons to life. Your life is very much like a day—morning, afternoon, evening—and you must know where you're at a particular time in your life.

There is no reason to try to act like you're in the morning if you're in the evening. Don't try to go back to your twenties when you are in your sixties. There is nothing worse than an old person trying to act young. Being old doesn't mean you have to be dried up, grumpy, and grouchy. You may be old, but you can be old and sweet, old and exciting, old and active. If you're older, be proud of your age, but remember that you're in your evening and not your morning.

There is also nothing worse than a young person trying to act old. Some young people need to go somewhere, sit down, and learn something. You don't know enough yet. There is some stuff you're not going to learn in school or in a book no matter how many degrees you have. There are some things you will only learn in the school of hard knocks and the college of experience.

Life is seasonal and you must know where you are and learn how to enjoy every season God allows you to have. Every period is different, necessary, and beneficial. Every period provides a learning process that brings you to the place where you can live to the glory of God. In the morning enjoy your youth, in the afternoon enjoy your years of maturity, and in the evening enjoy being older and thank God He let you live to see old age.

You need to be grateful that life has seasons and that each day is not the same. I know there are people who say that they wish their life stayed on an even keel. They wish things would mellow out, settle down, and less stressful. If life were like that, they would soon be bored out of their mind. Even people who live in Florida grow tired of the sunshine. God knows better than you that all sunshine may look good, but without rain nothing would grow. God sends seasons of sunshine and rain and while the sunshine may be nicer, the rain is still necessary. God knows you would never grow if He didn't send rain. In His wisdom and love, God balances your life with joy and sorrow, victory and defeat, mountains and valleys.

God gives balance. I didn't always understand this because I thought if God loved me, He would only give me mountaintop experiences. I soon learned that one of the ways God shows His love is by taking me from the mountain to the valley. I thought if God were really with me, my life would be one unbroken string of joy. I found out that God shows His love for me by mingling in some sorrow. I thought if God were really resident in me, I would have one continuous victory, only to discover that God allowed me to suffer some defeat. God knows that defeat, failure, and sorrow will bring balance to our lives.

Every now and then God will put you in the valley or allow you to experience failure, defeat, or trouble to balance you out. That keeps you humble and makes you realize that apart from Him you can do nothing. All of your help comes from Him: *"Not by might nor by power, but by my Spirit, says the Lord Almighty"* (Zechariah 4:6).

It is in the valley where you learn about God. You don't know how to worship until you have been through something. You don't know how to praise until you've been through something. You learn to bless God when you've fallen and don't know how you're going to get up. Have you ever been so weak that you didn't think you were going to make it and all of a sudden in your weakest, lowest moment you received strength that came from God? That is because God balances your life with both mountains and valleys and you learn to praise Him even in the valley.

Conclusion

WHEN I WAS GROWING up in Far Rockaway, New York, one of the first songs I remember our church choir singing was *In Holy Reverence Lord We Come* by D. Otis Teasley:

> In holy reverence, Lord, we come.
> Before thy throne this hour.
> To worship at thy hallowed feet.
> To sup the wine of joy so sweet.
> Great God of love and power.

I am much older now and I have been gone from New York longer than I lived there. I have known pain, loss, failure, and sorrow, but I still sing that song and believe it more now than ever, especially verse two:

> Our lives and all are in thy hands.
> Our times are known to thee.
> Thy grace has kept us thro' the past.
> Thy loving hands have held us fast.
> And shall eternally.

Time is a precious commodity that once used cannot be recovered. Learn how to master your time instead of allowing your time to master you. We all have the same twenty-four hours each day, and we all make decisions as to what we will do with those twenty-four hours. Don't waste time doing things that are outside your area of giftedness.

- Focus on your assignment. If you don't know what your assignment is, ask God.

- Set priorities for your time so that you will receive the greatest return on energy expended.

- Become competent in your area of giftedness. I recently heard a saying: "School is never out for the professional," which means you will always have something to learn. Become a professional student.

- Maximize your time so that you will fully and competently flow in your season.

God knows your times and seasons; now is a good season for you to begin *Making the Most of Your Time!*

Please enjoy this excerpt from
Living in the Blessed Place, ISBN 978-0-9764022-8-2.

There is a place in God where we move beyond a blessing to living a blessed life. It doesn't matter how old you are, how much in debt you are, or how many bad decisions you have made. If you have faith to believe that God is able to reverse your situation, then you, too, can start living the blessed life in the blessed place.

The blessed place is not reserved for super saints or those who have been pure all their lives. The blessed place is for people who live in the real world with real problems. We serve a God who is able to turn our mess into miracles. You may think it can't be that simple or easy, but it is. God has the power and He is no respecter of person, but He is a respecter of faith. Wherever God sees faith, He steps in, moves, and performs a miracle.

We don't like to talk about living in the blessed place because a few preachers have misused, misquoted, and misrepresented this teaching. We have stayed away from it lest we become lumped in with them. That is a trick of the devil. Just because some people abuse the teaching doesn't stop it from being true. When we fail to preach it, and then fail to live it, we deny the saints a powerful part of their inheritance as sons and daughters of God. The Bible says, *"My people are destroyed from lack of knowledge"* (Hosea 4:6).

It is not the will of God for His people to be ignorant. We have not taught the saints the fullness of their inheritance. Saints have died never experiencing the fullness of life that God, through Jesus Christ by the Holy Spirit, says they can have. We have put them in a spiritual straightjacket. Jesus came to give us life and that more abundantly. Enjoy your salvation. It is God's will to bless us, and when we don't walk in those blessings, we live short of God's best for us.

Some years ago I heard a story of what might happen to us when we get to heaven. According to the story, God will show us all the things that could and should have been ours; yet, we never believed nor asked for them. Now I know that story is not a biblical truth, but it helps to point out how far below our potential we often live.

Perhaps because of our background we tend to think that if we ask God for too much, we will bankrupt Him and heaven. We will never out-dream or out-do God in His abundance, His provision, and His desire to bless us. What God told Abram is what He says to us, "I will give you as far as you can see," and God sees us *Living in the Blessed Place!*

Other Books by
Bishop Timothy J. Clarke

Caution! God at Work—Trusting God through tough times

Celebrating the Family: Lessons from the Book of Ruth

Living in the Blessed Place

Making the Most of Your Time

The Price of Victory: Strategies for winning a faith fight

Reclaim Your Spiritual Health

To My Sisters Beloved: A trilogy of encouragement

www.ingramcontent.com/pod-product-compliance
Lightning Source LLC
Chambersburg PA
CBHW060520030426
42337CB00015B/1952